DIVERSE POEMS VOLUME I

RL
Literary productions

About the Book

The poems with Christian thematic were inspired by God and are for His glory.

Some romantic poems were inspired by my loved one Ana Carolina.

Table of Contents

UNIT I — Christian

The Bless of the Lord

God loves you and me,
With us until the end, the Lord will be.
He will never forget nor leave you,
Trust in Him is what you must do.

Trust quiet, with closed eyes,
He does your way better,
And He is always by our side.

Follow the path He leads you through,
Day and night, He will reward you,
With much love and blessings,
The Lord will rid you of all pains.

God enlightens you and changes your life,
Always for something better,
Deliver your life to Him,
The best for you will come from Him.

Always stay with God,
A great blessing will come,
He protects you from a dark destiny,
You will never be alone.

Be faithful, and everything will be right,
Always have the Lord on your side,
Then, alone, you will never be,
You will have great strength to continue.

Then, being always with the Lord,
He only wants your good and loves you,
Be calm and be faithful.
In the end, the Lord will save his chosen ones.
The eternal blessing, He will give in heaven.

The Upstairs

One upstairs, I am going up,
Each day, I go up a stair.
I try to do always good things,
Deviating me from all bad things.

The climb is not an easy way,
Many obstacles arise all day,
Even with all the difficulties, I know one thing.
I am not lonely.

There is someone who protects me,
He is always caring about my walk.
And if I discourage, He extends his hand,
Forever He will lift me high again.

He always lifts me higher,
He is driving me to victory.
God is always with me,
He is covering me with his glory.

The Glory of God in My Life

God, I am weak, and I need your power,
I want a big transformation in my life.
Your glory fulfilling my being is my desire.

My being shows your greatness,
My love will be dedicated to You,
May your presence in me be my greatest richness.

Your richness is more than everything,
To be free and happy with You is my biggest luxury.
Your rewards are more than this life here.

This world is only the beginning,
God has more for all of us,
He has great benefits.

One blessing, we could not imagine,
It will be a new life with abundant grace,
Where everyone will live to adore and see His face.

The Great Victory

On the day when I go the paradise,
I can see the face of the Lord, my Father.
I will contemplate his infinite glory,
I will be in my great victory.

A victory in Jesus Christ,
Living in the purer light.
Fulfilling the greatest promise:
To gain an eternal living.

An eternally, beautiful, and marvelous life,
Living in a celestial residence,
I am feeling your majestic presence.

Eternal majestic, splendid, and perfect.
On which in my life reigned,
And in eternity, delight me.

The Transformation of God

I want to see your greatness,
I want to watch You and see your glory.
I wait on You many blessings,
I hope You write me a new history.

Only your mercy can save the people,
For everyone, the Lord has many protections.
On our walking, You are ridding us of all evils,
Taking us to the right, in a good direction.

Our well, only the Lord who knows it.
He makes a way we do not understand it,
In each new way, a new stage is coming up,
And each stage we pass, we are growing up.

We grow mainly in the spiritual things,
God makes us people improved in everything,
People who avoid evil ways,
And seek truths on Sacred Scriptures' pages.

The Path with Jesus

Sometimes, I stay so sad,
It seems I am alone.
But I am not alone,
Jesus is with me in my path.

Jesus Christ is our Lord,
Lord of the world and redeemer,
Redeemer of all faithful people,
Besides the faithful, until the greatest sinner.

The sin destroys you,
Destroys your precious soul.
A soul with more value,
The value paid with blood,
Blood of Christ, our rescuer.

Only Jesus will save you,
Save from the perdition,
Perdition that is in the world,
A world full of destruction,
Destruction of the lives,
Lives that are thrown away,
Away from the plan of God,
God, who acts without delay.

God in everyone will act,
Act to change lives,
All life will be improved,
In all things, and your way will be transformed,
Transforming the failure into a very special victory,
A special victory because is very blessed,
Blessed, unique, and perfect.
Perfect because cannot be compared,
Compare with God is impossible,
Impossible because only He is unequaled.

Hallelujah

Sometimes we are so sad,
Many times, we question if God is there,
We think we are alone.
And for us, that is no one.
In this way, we shall not think,
Because to save us, God exists,
He comes and wants to hear us speak:
Hallelujah! Hallelujah! Hallelujah! Hallelujah!

Praise God with all your heart,
He will give us a great award.
Our blessings will be so immense.
God provides us with much recompense,
For Him gives it to us, we shall cry out:
Hallelujah! Hallelujah! Hallelujah! Hallelujah!

Let God guide your steps,
For you, He has the best.
He knows what we must do,
Knows how things should work for you.
God has one great plan for you,
To accomplish it, in Him, you need to believe.
Believe and never stop to adore Him.
Praise to God, and He will bless you in everything...
Hallelujah! Hallelujah! Hallelujah! Hallelujah!

Every time you praise Him,
On you will live the Holy Spirit.
God is present with you,
Your mouth will exalt Him,
The place will be filled with God's glory,
Hallelujah! Hallelujah! Hallelujah! Hallelujah!

Many wonders, God will operate,
Cures and miracles, He will make.
He will transform the lives of everyone,
The souls to paradise, He will guide.
In this awesome place,
Too many songs for Him, we will praise...
Hallelujah! Hallelujah! Hallelujah! Hallelujah!

When You Touch Me

I was so alone and tired,
I need someone to help me.
A light, a direction, a companion,
And always to be by my side.

Someone to help and teach me,
One who has patience and be my friend,
Leading me through the best way,
Doing things to my soul be saved.

There is only one person who can do this,
The Lord Jesus Christ. He is the King of kings.
When He touches me, He will change everything.
His blood has been poured for my sins to be forgiven.

With Christ, I am not alone,
I have the true light for my direction.
He will always guide me,
Out of His presence, I will never put myself away.
Because in eternity with Christ, I want to stay.

The Wonders of Jesus

I am here to adore You,
Because I know my life can be changed by You,
All evils, He will put to an end,
Happiness and joy will reign.

Jesus Christ is my Lord!
He loves me and treats me with love,
Jesus desires my praise.
I open my mouth, and His name, I proclaim:
Jesus is my Lord, and He is amazing!

By my side, Jesus is always with me,
To see my ways and lead me.
Because He knows the best way to go,
He is with me, in the best way, He is leading me.

In Jesus, I put my faith and trust,
And He always keeps me standing.
To save my soul and make me happy, He is desiring,
To me, God is watching.
Hearing my voice while I am praying,
He knows what I am seeking.
And my life, He is changing.

In my life, God is acting,
From all evils, He is protecting me.
Because the Holy Spirit will cover me.
The Holy Spirit acts in a special way,
He covers and protects me from evil every day.
Under his awesome protection, I stay,
I follow loving God in an unconditional way.

God Sees Everything

Lord God, in a marvelous celestial throne you are sitting,
One throne on which blessings irradiate.
In this throne, the whole Earth, He is seeing.

The Lord sees, hears, and knows everything.
Nothing that happens can escape from Him.
Only the Lord God is in the entire world.

A world that seems does not have a course,
Very confused and weak, people are wandering.
Of His grace, everyone is needing.

The Lord is the one who has the true power,
This power transforms all and everything.
To happen, we need to obey and believe in Him.

This is God, the Lord!

Do not think you can go alone,
You need someone.
Then, your life will improve.
In a good destiny, God will lead you.
This is God, the Lord!
He loves you so much.

He does good things to you,
Through true paths, He leads you,
It is that enough you accept Him.
The change in your life will begin,
He will give you many things:
A great love!
He will heal you!
He will save you,
He is God, the Lord!

If you get discouraged someday,
On your side, the Lord will stay.
Giving you strength and determination.
Holding your hand in any situation,
He is God, the Lord!

Do not deny nor reject Him!
He wants you to accept Him!

The change will come your way,
Your world, He will transform each day,
You only need to accept Him,
Your world will improve in everything,
He is God, the Lord!

Do not think you are alone,
For your path, God has the best one,
He is God, the Lord!

As you could notice,
Everything in your life improved when He entered.
Your destiny could be transformed,
Accept Him in your heart.
Hold his hands and do not go apart.
He is God, the Lord!

Thank You

Thank you, my Lord, for my life,
All days the Lord blesses me,
There are many blessings I receive.

Thank you for my way,
Because the Lord leads me forever,
And You make me wake up all day.

Thank you for my food.
My pantry, the Lord is filling,
I have no lack of anything.

Thank you for being merciful,
Because You looked on me,
And have saved me from a world dreadful.

Thank you for your forgiveness.
He freed me from the wrath and punishment,
And gave me a new heart.

Thank you for loving me,
A love that is big and marvelous,
That eternal life will give me.

Jesus

Look on high,
Get up your head,
And see that light.
It is the biggest purity that exists,
That one is Jesus!
He has immense power,
And everything He can do.
Look on the sick, it was cured,
The paralyzed one walks,
Jesus makes all this,
For whom love Him.

You do not need to be rich,
To be famous or renowned,
Jesus just wants your faith.
And from your heart, He must be adored.
Follow his steps,
And your life will change for the better.
Jesus is the only path,
And good things will give you.

The path seems hard to do,
But it is not!
See to the blessings,
And fortify your faith.
To the Father, you shall obey,
Because for who fear Him.
The victories are coming.

Stay tuned!
Only Jesus is the way, the truth, and the life!
Other ways may exist,
But no one has the true light,
That is Jesus!
Who died on the cross for us.
He gave his blood,
And for Him, it was so painful,
He made everything as proof of love.

Follow the great shepherd,
To be a winner.
The world wants to deceive you,
Easy and wrong things are shown to do,
Trying to charm you.
Do not fall into this trap!
Because who gets out of the light,
Has great troubles in his life.

But if you get out of the light,
For that, you can come back again.
Repent of what you made,
And for God, you will be forgiven.

With the forgiveness gained,
Do not go, and get out of the way,
Because the trap is big.
And you cannot escape one day.
Always stay with God,
In the best path.
So, you will smile every day.

Only God is the Way

One star will indicate a way, a direction,
This direction is God,
In your life, God will make a transformation.

After being transformed, you will be modified,
With old things, you no longer stay satisfied.
Your salve time has finished,
And now, everything is renewed.

After the renovation, there is only a path to follow…
God!
You will get the best with the Lord.

You never must stop dreaming,
Have faith in God, and you will realize many things.
Be happy and go ahead,
In your mind, have only goodness.

With the stars, God will guide you,
And He will say:
Go ahead in my faith.

Some people will try to deviate you,
Never give up because God will never let you.
Go ahead, and other people, try to change them,
With your help, the world may be excellent.

By a divine light, you will be touched,
It will be God saying to continue.
Never give up the fight,
Because the Lord always will be on your side.

Many things have already been transformed,
On your side, every time you have the Lord.
Go ahead and show to the world,
The true path is God.
And a new destiny will be performed,
With much love and peace,
With everything wrong, we will finish...

What I Really Need

I do not need a superhero,
I need a Savior.
To change my being,
Because a hero cannot do anything.

I do not need fame and fortune,
I need your glory.
Because with it, I will write a new story.

I do not live without my best friend,
He is a perfect person.
He always loves me and will be with me until the end.

I love the power of God,
His power is the purest love.
I feel many blessings,
From the hand of God, they are coming.

I desire many good days with Jesus Christ,
So, I have new paths in my life.

The Lion of the Tribe of Judah

The Lion of the tribe of Judah.
Sat down on a magnificent throne, He is.
With quick eyes, He contemplates everything.
Your power and strength are without limits.

Your majestic is very great,
With his imposing roar, the evil was chased away.
And with his claws, Satan is smashed,
Letting him down on the ground and humiliated.

For whom are faithful, He protects with his right hand,
Fight all kinds of battles for them.
Getting away from all evils, all wrath, all envy,
Throwing away all bad things.

In your throne, I do my refugee,
In your shadow, I rest and have peace.
Waiting for the day of your glory,
Doing my heart meek.

Change of Life

One day, I was lost,
In many ways, I was walking,
But I found nothing and have nothing.
It seemed to have many people around me,
But in the end, I was lonely.

I thought everything was correct,
I thought my way was perfect,
I was cheated many times on this path.
Everyone laughed about me,
And I feel completely humiliated.

One day, my life has changed,
There was one person who believed in me.
And everything was different...
Jesus Christ came to meet me,
He changed my sad history.

After God has rescued me,
I can walk in the presence of the King.
And many obstacles, I could overcome,
Because for God, there are no limits.

One Blessing

Oh, Lord! I am a big sinner,
I am not worthy of your infinite grace.
But even with all my mistakes,
The high One came and blessed me.

There was not a small blessing.
The greater one has come in my life.
One blessing with the taste of victory,
At the perfect moment, it came and changed my history.

A history of weeping and supplications.
Weeping poured almost all day.
Tireless supplications, your favor, I was seeking.
Many times, I asked You, your grace, I was waiting.

On the day of my anguish and desperation, I was blessed.
A great and unexpected blessing came to me.
The supplication has been heard, and the weep was dried.
Now with the great blessing, I am in a new life.

The Way

In many ways, you can follow,
However, just one will serve you.
It is the way that saves you,
It is the way the Lord leads you.

I was very confused one day,
Very convinced, I was walking in my way.
Convinced that my way was correct,
But this way was not perfect.

Then, one day, God touched me,
He showed me, and the right way, I could see.
One way with peace and happiness,
And his blessings are endless.

This is the way of the Lord,
That is full of love.
God will give you the better,
From all evils, you will be protected.

The enemy will tempt you.
To the wrong path, he will try to lead you.
Do not fall into this trap,
Because he wants to destroy your life.
Always follow with God,
Because He protects his people.

God leads us to the better,
He saves our lives today and forever.
His ways are eternal,
They are far from hell.

God leads us to paradise,
His ways have too much light.
Follow Him to save your life,
And forever, you will live in paradise.

UNIT II — Diverse

Roses

One rose may be of any color type,
Some are blue, red, or even white,
However, all have a thing in the essence:
The incomparable beauty and the love's presence.

A rose can be live and radiant,
Or can be dry and without color.
But one thing will never change,
The rose will never produce pain.

Roses go, roses come.
And always making happy someone,
She may be in light color,
Or in a dark coloring,
And always its tenderness is showing.

Unfortunately, one day the rose withers,
And its beauty is over...
But it cannot happen one thing:
The end of the love,
Just because there is no rose,
To symbolize it.

Reason and Heart

Many things happen,
Without noticing it.
However, another only happens if you allow it.

You cannot control,
In a thing, you cannot see,
The heart is one of them,
When you are not expecting,
A new love, he is bringing.

You will fight against that thing!
But you have no chance of winning!
Your heart always controls everything.

The reason will say do not try,
The heart will fight.
A dilemma will be generated…
And the step for the solution,
It will be very complicated.

The heart will say yes!
The reason will say no!
And who will I listen to?
To the heart or the reason?

Wrong Choices

A choice can change everything,
One unique word,
It can destroy a world,
Or can build a future.

It is not easy to do an election,
We can choose the worst direction.
And someone very important can lose.

You can even make a mistake.
The mistake can be fatal.
Leading you to a sad final.

The mistake can be erased,
Solving everything wrong.
In this way, even love can be reconciled.

Dreams

Dreams, all of us have,
Some dreams will be followed,
And others can only be dreamed.

Even thinking about your dream,
Or fighting to make it come true.
Everything you can, you must do.

To paradise, a dream can lead you,
But in the blink of an eye,
At rock bottom, you will arrive.

Always be very careful,
In your fight for a dream,
Of crazy one, people can call you.
Do not hear anybody! Go ahead!
And see your dream come true.

UNIT III — Romantic

Mute Lover

The mute lover is that one who exists,
He always keeps close to the beloved person,
Only observing his beloved one.

He tries to speak!
But never do it...
He fears making a mistake,
And his beautiful love goes away.

When he feels these feelings,
His conscience says:
Declare everything and be happy. No more waiting.

When the mute lover says something,
His whole world can change,
And can make real all his dreams.

The mute lover continues to think,
Wondering what to do...
Who knows one day,
It will happen some attitude...

Love

If to love was a crime,
Many people would be seized,
Is there something better than by love be accompanied?

With a love, everything changes, each gesture and action.
Always doing all for the beloved person,
And proportioning a new emotion.

The love is mysterious,
Sometimes simple, almost silent.
Even so, it will always be a feeling so magnificent.

With love, the paradise, you can reach.
In a great kiss or simply in one see,
Each time, the love increases.

If one day, the love will go away. What to do?
Only regretting? Or to make something?
To get it back and be happy.

The Color of the Love

If love were a color, what would it be?
It could be white,
Where all runs calmly.

It could be blue,
A strong thing,
But with a touch of purity.

It could be red,
Always fiery,
And very intense.

It could be green,
Always renewing,
The hope of happiness.

It could be pink,
Always delicate,
And very present.

It could be yellow,
Always lightening,
And charming everyone.

It could be dark,
Always enigmatic,
And very mysterious.

It could be a rainbow,
Always full of surprises,
And appearing in unexpected places.

Love does not need color to symbolize it,
For itself, he is wonderful.
If it was a color, it would not be funny.
Because it always would be the same thing.
The love is always changing,
Always transforming,
And each day is renewing.

In this rhyme of renewing,
One day, without notice,
Someone, you are loving...

Your Presence

Pass through you,
Without observing you and amazing me,
It is foolish, or better, it is impossible!

When I see you, then, I think:
How to contain me?
And do not say to you,
How much I admire you.

When I am close to you,
Everything stays beautiful.
When I go away,
With you, the beauty stays.

When I say goodbye,
I think next time.
When I see you again,
And everything stays beautiful again.

Inevitable Thought

How do not think about you,
If when I close my eyes,
I see you in my thoughts.

Thoughts that get lost...
When I open my eyes,
If I see you, everything is fine.

But when I do not see,
I close my eyes again,
To see you wonderful again.

To continue seeing you wonderful,
And to feel you too,
All my love, I promise you.

Indescribable

It is impossible to describe you.
If I wrote thousands of pages,
I could not say,
How much I admire you.

A million of praises,
It would be a little,
To demonstrate your beauty.

You always charm me,
It can be speaking, or just,
On a simple smile.

Some stars shine,
Others, even more.
And you will be,
The most beautiful girl in my sight.

New Feelings

When I met you,
I just wanted to be your friend,
But today, more than this, I pretend.

I do not know how,
I do not know the cause!
I just know that happened.

A chance is what I want,
To demonstrate what I feel for you.
Then, you may notice,
You have the same feeling too.

Incomparable Beauty

An incomparable person you are,
With a unique beauty. Your sweet smile,
This turns you into an unforgotten woman.

Your eyes, two pearls, intensely bright.
It does who is close to you,
Do not stop to watch.

Your face, so sweet, beautiful, and delightful,
When I look at it, I think: how wonderful!

For you, an entire day, I can watch,
At the end of this day, satisfied, I will be.
Because I know; that if I fall in love,
It was for a wonderful woman I did see.

Your Passing

When you pass,
It is not impossible to not notice.
You are so gracious,
That holds my view.

Looking at you, I turn off the rest,
My thoughts stay lost...
But soon, they met themselves on you.

When you go away, I am sad.
But I remember you will pass again,
It will make me happy.

Feelings

The feelings appear,
Sometimes, unexpectedly.
We do not notice, and we begin,
To like somebody.

This person may be close to,
Or even if far.
But that does not matter,
It does not change the feeling.

My feelings for you,
Also started in this way.
Even if you are far away,
It has not changed, stayed strong.

In our meeting, I ask you for a chance,
To demonstrate it and win you over.

Strong Desire

My beloved one, each time I see you,
I feel a big desire to have you.

A desire to hug you,
Kiss you, to have you close to me.
Doing my heart beats faster.

Because he beats faster for you,
He wants you to calm him.
With your delicacy and kindness,
You can give him a bit of happiness.

On Your Side

You enlighten my day,
On your side, I can have sweet dreams.
My reality is better than a dream!
I can love you.

A strong love, pretty and delightful.
That makes me always love you,
A love that overcomes barriers,
Because it is a wonderful love.

I really love you,
I do not want to stay without you.
When we are separated,
My heart almost dies missing you.

On your side, for a long, I want to stay,
I love you today, tomorrow, and all day!
There is nothing better than loving you,
There is nothing better than being close to you.

Special

You are very special!
You do not need to do anything,
You do not need to say anything,
You are special because you exist.

Your existence makes you graceful,
Your presence makes you unequaled.
For yourself, you are wonderful.

So wonderful, that I do not stop to watch,
I stay fixed on you to admire you.
Sincere admiration, depth admiration.
That makes me write to express my appreciation.

For you, too many written words would be necessary,
You deserve this, and much more,
Because you are very special to me.

The Chocolate

The chocolate is sweet and delicious,
But there is something better,
Your kiss is more luscious.

One passionate and attractive kiss.
After trying it once, that wonderful sensation,
Never gets out of my mind.

A sensation so wonderful,
That makes me desire more.
I want to have you,
I want to kiss you.

More than kisses, I want to give you,
A true love, I have for you.
And for you, I have a too special way,
With too much love all day.

Thoughts

When I am with you,
I have only a thought: You!
When I am not with you,
I have only a thought: You!

You are always in all my thoughts,
The whole time, I think about you,
Good and wonderful thoughts!
To think about my love is great.

Better than thinking is to be with you!
Hugging, kissing, and feeling you.
Then, I can show you my love.

I give you my love in the manner of affection,
Be sure that is sincere love,
Strength love, from the bottom of my heart.
I want that love to last for a long time.

For You

What to say about you?
I could say you are pretty, wonderful,
You are very special, but this…
I think you already know it.

What can I think about you?
I could think I adore you,
I like you very much,
Or I only could think about you.
Because you are everything!

What to do for you?
I could do everything to please you,
Do everything to make you happier.
Then, to do everything for you…

You

Among all I met,
You are the prettier,
Your look, your face...
You are wonderful.

It can be speaking,
Even in silence.
You are always so gracious.

You are everything!
No one can compare with you.
Your beauty is the maximum in my view.

Confused

I am very confused,
I do not know what to do or what to say,
I do not know what to think.

Sometimes, I stop to think,
Thoughts that go, and they get lost...
Thoughts lost, without direction.
They have no direction or instruction.

I would like to know what to do!
I would like to know what to say!
I would like to know how to do it!

I am so because I am a victim of passion.
One passion that destroys me,
One passion that disorients me.
This passion charmed me,
My biggest desire is always to have this passion,
So, I can be happy.

Love not Loved

What to do with my feelings?
Who will I give them to?
Who will want them?

I would like to give them to you,
I would like these feelings to be yours.
I would like you to accept me,
I would like you to love me.

My love already has an owner,
The owner is you.
You are the owner of my heart.

A love that pulsates strongly for you,
A feeling that wants you with me,
I am falling in love with you.

The Love and the Time

The time is passing,
The more time passes,
The more I think about you,
And you, more, I am loving.

My love grows all day,
My affection is always rising.
What I feel is real!
You are always in my feelings.

Your love is what I need,
Your affection is what I wish,
Your presence is my desire,
I want to hug you and feel your lips.

Never let me, always stay with me.
Be sure I have much love to give you.
Feel my heart when I say: I love you!
Because you are the unique person I want to love.

To Love

To love someone is not easy,
To win the beloved person is hard.
The love, in many ways, can be shown,
And the beloved person will be won.

This person will rejoice,
They will say everything is very exciting.
She will be right in her statement,
Love comes from the heart.

With you, my heart wants to stay,
To love you, give you much affection.
My heart wants your love next to him,
To be very happy.

One Kiss

One kiss can change everything,
The passion can ignite,
And increases many feelings.

With one kiss, in paradise, one can arrive,
Because there are always wonderful sensations.
Rising wonderful feelings and emotions,
He makes me feel the taste of love.

It is good your love's savor,
Even better, it is your kiss,
It gives my life a delicious flavor.

This flavor is so good, and forever, I want to have it.
One thing is necessary for this,
It needs to have you with me.

Enchanting

How do not enchant me,
For a person so pretty.
With unique beauty,
You left me in awe when I was looking.

When I look, I stay thinking:
How I want to love you!
With you, I want to stay.

I can have you,
For my love, I will demonstrate,
And I will make you smile all day.

Better Love

Since the first time, I saw you,
Something special, I notice,
You are wonderful and beautiful.

When I talked to you,
One hope, I could have.
Then, I was a little closer to you.

I noticed you were very special,
One day, I took one attitude.
And it is worth it,
Your kiss was my incredible final.

This kiss leads us to a dating,
With a beautiful and wonderful love,
We will get married one day.

You II

When I see you,
My day gets illuminated,
When I think about you,
My mind gets fascinated.

I could say too much about of you,
To write too many words to praise you.
But there are three words to mention:
Beautiful, wonderful, special.

Beautiful, a stunning beauty.
Wonderful, an incredible woman.
Special, sensible, and sweet.

Your Love

Not to love you is impossible,
Staying without you is unthinkable.
With your love, everything is good and wonderful.

One marvel that I love very much.
One good feeling that I adore it.
On your side, I feel special,
With you, I want to be the whole time.

Stay together you, to hug and love you,
Giving you too much love and affection.
Because I am falling in love with you,
And with you, for a long time, I want to be.

My Love

You are my passion,
It is the woman that I love.
You are perfect, beautiful, wonderful,
You are the owner of my heart and emotions.

Every night I dream with your kiss,
The more time passes,
The more my desire for you increases.

I want to hug you,
I want to kiss you.
I have a big will,
That makes me want to love you.

I love you much,
I want you always,
Always on my side.

About the Author

Rafael Henrique dos Santos Lima

Associate Degree in Administration and M.B.A. in Strategic Project Management by Centro Universitário UNA. Christian by the grace of God. Passionate about writing (English, Portuguese, Spanish), poet and novelist.

Contacts

rafael50001@hotmail.com

rafaelhsts@gmail.com

Blog: escritorrafaellima.blogspot.com

Acknowledgements

I thank my wife who is an amazing inspiration in my life.

The following websites contain significant useful information for writing the book.

Google Docs

Google Translator

Grammarly

RhymeZone

Special Acknowledgement

I thank God. He gave me the intelligence to write the book.